blue
rider
press

Walter Potter's Curious World of Taxidermy

WALTER POTTER'S CURIOUS WORLD OF TAXIDERMY

DR. PAT MORRIS

with JOANNA EBENSTEIN

BLUE RIDER PRESS

a member of Penguin Group (USA)

New York

blue
rider
press

Published by the Penguin Group
Penguin Group (USA) LLC
375 Hudson Street
New York, New York 10014

USA · Canada · UK · Ireland · Australia
New Zealand · India · South Africa · China

penguin.com
A Penguin Random House Company

First published in the UK in 2008 by MPM Publishing; substantially revised edition with new photographs
published in 2013 in the UK by Constable, an imprint of Constable Robinson LTD.
Copyright © 2014 by P. A. Morris

Library of Congress Cataloging-in-Publication Data

Morris, Pat, date.
Walter Potter's curious world of taxidermy / by Dr. Pat Morris with Joanna Ebenstein.
p.   cm.
ISBN 978-0-399-16944-1
1. Potter, Walter, 1835–1918.   2. Potter's Museum of Curiosity.
3. Taxidermists—England—Biography.   I. Title.
QL31.P686M67   2014   2013042632
590.75'2—dc23

Printed in China
1 3 5 7 9 10 8 6 4 2

Book design by Gretchen Achilles

CONTENTS

FOREWORD

In 2010, the legendary pop artist Sir Peter Blake co-curated an exhibition at Primrose Hill's Museum of Everything in London. This was the first time a number of pieces by the Victorian taxidermist Walter Potter had been exhibited together since the collection—which had been on view for nearly 150 years—was broken up at auction in 2003. The exhibition drew more than 30,000 visitors in six weeks and attracted enthusiastic coverage in the press.

One day in the late 1950s, when I was about fifteen, I went on a cycling holiday with my father. We stopped at a pub in the village of Bramber, noticed the little museum across the road, and, inquisitive, decided we should visit. That was fifty-five years ago, but I still remember walking into a space like a dusty Boy Scout hut, filled with wondrous things.

I never returned to Bramber, and some years later I read that Mr. Potter's Museum of Curiosity was to be sold. After briefly entertaining the idea of trying to buy it, I realized I would have nowhere to install it and, more pertinent, I had no money. I didn't see the museum at its new homes in Brighton or Arundel, but caught up with it once more in Cornwall, by coincidence just before I read again that its contents were for sale.

Damien Hirst was rumored to have offered a million pounds for the entire collection, and that would have been perfect if it had been installed in his planned museum and gallery at Toddington Manor, but it wasn't to be.

So on Tuesday, September 23, 2003, I arrived at Jamaica Inn for the two-day auction. I was surprised that Damien wasn't there, but I recognized some old friends, the art dealer James Birch and the photographer David Bailey. I was told recently that the television personality Harry Hill was also there.

My plan was to buy enough pieces to re-create, within my own collection, a small version of Mr. Potter's Museum of Curiosity. I allocated £10,000, beyond which I wouldn't go; I think I eventually spent £10,100.

Lot 13 was *The Death & Burial of Cock Robin*. As Mr. Potter's first tableau, and arguably the best item in the auction, this sold for £20,000, and my hopes of getting very much were severely dented. Fate was perhaps on my side, though: during bidding on *House That Jack Built*, a car backfired outside, sounding like gunshot, and bidding stopped at my offer of £3,200; so I acquired what I consider Mr. Potter's second-best tableau. Further items were added to my collection, including *The Babes in the Wood*. I have made my own version of Mr. Potter's museum and ten years after the auction still enjoy it very much.

Peter Blake

1 May 2013, London

MUSEUM

OPEN · DAILY

BRAMBER MUSEUM.

CHAPTER 1

THE LIFE & TIMES OF WALTER POTTER

Walter Potter was born on July 2, 1835. He spent all of his long life in the West Sussex village of Bramber, where he still rests in the churchyard. A distinctive and bewhiskered man, he dressed in a three-piece suit, with a silver watch chain dangling from his waistcoat pocket, and a white straw boater hat in summer. He always wore a top hat to church on Sundays; he served as a warden for thirty years and a parish overseer for even longer. In later life he spent his leisure time carefully tending his garden, where he worked long hours and grew flowers for sale.

Potter in 1880, winding cotton threads around a mounted sparrowhawk to hold its feathers in place while the skin dried. The false body would have been made from the bundle of wood wool.

The Original Death & Burial Of Cock Robin

CHAPTER 2

TABLEAUX

The anthropomorphic tableaux—cases of stuffed animals arranged in human scenes—were the most famous and distinctive items in Potter's tiny museum; but for these, he and his collection would have been forgotten long ago. Today they show us what some aspects of Victorian life would have looked like, and in Potter's day many people would have instantly recognized the scenes. There is no question that the tableaux, as social commentaries, were both original and intriguing when they were first exhibited. Only later would ambiguity develop in people's reactions to what they saw before them.

The Kittens' Wedding, *with glass removed, in situ at Bramber Museum.*

THE KITTENS' WEDDING

THE KITTENS' WEDDING

CIRCA 1890

24 x 37 x 22 INCHES

In *The Kittens' Wedding*, made in the 1890s, most of the twenty kittens wear little morning suits or brocade dresses, and even frilly knickers (these are not visible). The clothes were made by one of Potter's neighbors and by his daughter Minnie. This was the last tableau completed by Potter, and the only one in which the animals are fully dressed. The case was always one of the most popular in the collection and was occasionally lent out for exhibitions at other museums (including the Victoria and Albert Museum and Liverpool Museum), as it was also the smallest of the major tableaux and therefore the most easily moved.

On this solemn occasion, the bride wears a long veil and carries a posy of orange blossom. She and the chief bridesmaid may be sisters, as they are similar in color, as is their younger brother, who wears a sailor's uniform (a popular type of dress for young boys, even if they were obviously not in the navy). A feline vicar in white surplice watches patiently as the bridegroom, with head tilted intently to one side, places a golden ring on his bride's finger. The vicar has his book open at the page showing "Will thou take this man . . ." A male kitten standing grumpily to one side had his open at a different page; he seems lost in thought, perhaps about his own relationship with the bride or his disapproval of the groom. Sadly, his little book has been lost.

The Death & Burial of Cock Robin

1861

62 x 74 x 20 inches

The *Death & Burial of Cock Robin* case is a little over two yards wide and took Potter seven years to build in his spare time. It features nearly one hundred British birds, some shown crying glass tears. Four species are included that are now rare or extinct in Sussex (red-backed shrike, cirl bunting, wryneck, hawfinch); there are also several canaries among other species. All but one of the poem's fourteen verses are depicted, the missing one referring to the kite ("Who'll carry the coffin? / I, said the kite, / if it's not through the night, / I'll carry the coffin"). This species would have been difficult to obtain in nineteenth-century Sussex and awkwardly large among the other birds.

Otherwise, all the characters are present: the infamous sparrow is there with his bow and arrow, the rook with his book, and the fish with his dish, just as in Jane Potter's book of nursery rhymes that had inspired her brother to build this churchyard scene. The church itself, painted in oil on the back board, shows the stone construction typical of such buildings in the Weald of Kent and Sussex. The chief mourner (a turtle dove) is followed poignantly by an adult robin (Mrs. Cock Robin, perhaps?) and three young ones. The solemn cortège extends down the church path, through the gate, and up to the church. It stretches back under an arch on the left, where a small mirror creates the illusion of other mourners in the distance.

The original nursery rhyme speaks of carrying "the link," a scepter-like item of funereal significance used in Victorian

*The rhyme as it appears on the case
is set out here:*

(from left to right)

Who killed Cock Robin?
I, said the Sparrow;
With my bow and arrow,
I killed Cock Robin

Who saw him die?
I, said the Fly,
With my little eye,
I saw him die.

Who caught his blood?
I, said the Fish,
With my little dish,
I caught his blood.

Who made his shroud?
I, said the Beetle;
With my little needle,
I made his shroud.

Who'll bear the pall?
We, said the Wrens,
Both Cock and Hen,
We'll bear the Pall.

Who'll dig the grave?
I, said the Owl;
With my spade and shovel,
I'll dig his grave.

(from left to right)

Who will carry the link?
I, said the Linnet,
I'll fetch it in a minute,
I will carry the link.

Who will be the chief mourner?
I, said the Dove,
For I mourn for my love,
I will be chief mourner.

Who will sing a psalm?
I, said the Thrush,
As I sit in the bush,
I will sing a psalm.

Who'll be the parson?
I, said the Rook,
With my little book,
I will be the parson.

Who'll be the clerk?
I, said the Lark,
If it's not in the dark,
I will be the clerk.

Who will toll the bell?
I, said the Bull,
Because I can pull.
So Cock Robin, farewell.

Then four of the party
Soon bore him away,
And so sadly ended
Cock Robin's unfortunate day.

A brambling and a bullfinch
(together with a sparrow and a redstart, out of sight)
carry the coffin on their shoulders.
Cock Robin's fatal wound is also visible.

Rabbits' Village School

CIRCA 1888

42 x 73 x 20 inches

Potter wanted fifty baby rabbits for *Rabbits' Village School*, but after asking around in local villages, he could get only the forty-eight that are here engaged in scholastic activities. The pupils are all about a month old, the teachers somewhat older. Potter made all the slates (from paper), pencils, and furniture himself, but asked his wife, Ann, to make the tiny clothes seen in the needlework class. The inkwells were carved from sticks of chalk. Four classes are shown in progress, sometime in 1888, as indicated on the class registers. A pupil in the writing class has blotted his copybook and is standing on the bench in tears, probably having been caned for his carelessness. One of his neighbors watches derisively or is

it sympathetically? A door is ajar, and a small rabbit creeps unobtrusively into the room, perhaps returning from a trip to the lavatory.

The girls in the sewing class include one who has darned the heel of a sock and is proudly showing it to her neighbor, while others inspect the stitching in a red petticoat. Another group stands reading a book about the opening of Westminster Bridge in 1862. One member of this group turns to help a friend who is struggling with his arithmetic. A rabbit at the back of the class has his hand raised in an effort to attract the teacher's attention. There is some consultation in the math class, where the rabbits wrestle with the challenges of addition and division. They are busily writing in chalk on their tiny wooden-framed slates. One has his sum wrong and is in disgrace; another tentatively shows his work to the teacher. Another rabbit is still sharpening his pencil, perhaps to avoid doing his computations. The school monitor is putting away the class register in a tall desk. A cane hangs menacingly on the wall below the clock, a silent warning to any who might misbehave.

These tiny rabbits, deeply engaged in their schoolwork, personify youthful innocence. The scene reflects typical school life for children in late Victorian times, similar to what a young Walter Potter himself would have experienced, perhaps in the very same village school that he visited to gain inspiration for this case.

THE UPPER TEN

CIRCA 1880 ❧ 39 x 74 x 21 INCHES

Potter made another large tableau about two yards wide and a yard high, *The Upper Ten*, depicting a squirrels' club, and a smaller one, *The Lower Five*, depicting a rats' den (the titles of these scenes were taken from a popular song of the day). These tableaux were keenly observed social commentaries with a clear class distinction between the two scenes and their animal occupants. Together with the eighteen toffs in the squirrels' club, some with expanded waistlines, are a servant bringing champagne and drinks on a tray and a junior offering a nut to his lordly superiors. There are cases of stuffed birds on the wall and spittoons on the floor. Two club members are engaged in a quiet game of cribbage. Another pair are in earnest discussion over whether to play the queen of diamonds at the card table, unaware that the squirrel opposite holds the jack and the king.

Other club members endlessly dispute some matter over a decanter of port. One, hand on hip and foot on chair, conducts an animated exchange with another, who taps the table with his fingertips and drops ash from his cigar. Potter added these two characters after seeing a newspaper picture depicting men in similar attitudes. The animals are all crudely stuffed, with no modeling under the skin to assist in creating details of expression. Yet these squirrels manage to convey a real sense of engagement and achieve extraordinary renditions of human behavior through their minutely observed postures. As with other cases, red squirrels are used because this was the "common squirrel" at the time, and many were shot as destructive pests by local foresters and gamekeepers.

THE LOWER FIVE

LATE NINETEENTH CENTURY

33 x 55 x 17 INCHES

In contrast to the squirrels' club, *The Lower Five* shows a rather scruffy rats' den. It is depicted as being raided by the local policemen, who see money on the table—clear evidence of wicked gambling over a game of dominoes. One player protests the way the game has gone, probably because his opponent has just laid the double six to claim the game in triumph. Among the fifteen rats, an injured one hobbles across the room, perhaps only recently escaped from a trap or a fight, and some of his associates appear to have drunk too much. One of the rats puzzles over what seems to be a set of instructions for filling in a census form. This might have been on Potter's mind: once he became head of the family, he was responsible for completing census returns every ten years from 1861 onward. He may well have found it tiresome, and the baffled rat represents a fellow sufferer. Other rats read or argue with one another or simply sleep. There seems to be a bit of a brawl on the right, attracting attention from the policeman at the door, although a tiny reassuring notice on the bench reads: "I've never seen that constable run a man in."

Potter made the furniture from cigar boxes; the tiny pictures he hung on the wall are old views of Bramber in spring and autumn. The rats in this den were caught locally for Potter by Spot, a friend's dog, when corn ricks were being dismantled at threshing time. They appear to have had their faces flattened, for a more human expression, with eyes facing more forward than out to the sides. This tends to reduce or eliminate the sinister pointed-nose appearance of living rats that people so dislike.

A player lays a double-six domino to win the game.

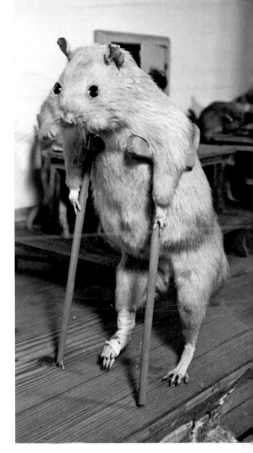

HAPPY FAMILY

CIRCA 1870

67 x 78 x 27 INCHES

Happy Family incorporated a variety of improbably associated animals. This reflects a Christian theme popular in Victorian art, where predators and their various prey were portrayed living together in harmony (among the best-known examples of this are Edward Hicks's various versions of *The Peaceable Kingdom*). Here, the cat, with a robin perched on its head, lies beside a dog, while rabbits play in front of a stoat, mice frolic under the gaze of owls, and falcons peacefully cohabit with small passerines. The idea was that Nature was not always "red in tooth and claw," but could also be gentle and friendly—a comforting reassurance (to children especially) that animals were nice creatures, just as in the books that inspired much of Potter's taxidermy. *Happy Family* also gave Potter an opportunity to use an assortment of spare taxidermy specimens, including various wild birds, a monkey, canaries, and a parrot. A small black rabbit, a tortoise, and a toad have joined this friendly scene.

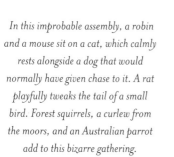

In this improbable assembly, a robin and a mouse sit on a cat, which calmly rests alongside a dog that would normally have given chase to it. A rat playfully tweaks the tail of a small bird. Forest squirrels, a curlew from the moors, and an Australian parrot add to this bizarre gathering.

A FRIEND IN NEED
IS A
FRIEND INDEED.

HOUSE THAT JACK BUILT

LATE NINETEENTH CENTURY

76 x 26 x 65 INCHES

This is the cock that crowed in the morn, that waked the priest all
shaven and shorn, that married the man all tattered and torn,
that kissed the maiden all forlorn, that milked the cow with the
crumpled horn, that tossed the dog, that worried the cat, that
killed the rat, that ate the malt that lay in the house that Jack built.

In *House That Jack Built*, Potter depicted all the characters in the popular nursery rhyme. The building was modeled on a local mill, and a sheaf of bills hangs inside one window of the malt house (where grain was allowed to partially germinate before being made into beer). Some grain spills from a leaking sack by the hoist, all ready for the rat to eat it, as the poem says.

The miniature cockerel was made by gluing feathers to a small model. The cow was a soft toy that Potter purchased; he stretched calfskin over it, and replaced the original button eyes with glass ones. The horns were formed from the tips of real horns. The tiny eggs in the farmyard chicken's nest are actually wren eggs.

In *Sporting*
tableaux, f
out ferreti
rabbits we
ing them f
cooking p
for some
many. Ta
to the war
and cause
have set
warren, b
come out
pers away
to shoot i
not to fir
back dov
would be
then be

to shoot their rabbits. One man (kneeling and with raised arm) has the name "Charles Charman" on his ferret bag, along with the date when the case was completed (1877). Charman was a friend of Potter's and owned Spot the dog, who caught the rats used in *The Lower Five* and whose miniature look-alike stands alert near her tiny master in this tableau, ready to seize any rabbits that might otherwise escape.

THE KINGFISHER
RIVER BANK

CIRCA 1878

54 x 40 x 14 INCHES

In *The Kingfisher River Bank*, Potter composed a large scene around kingfishers that he had found locally. He had watched the birds for a few days and managed to get a whole nest out of a burrow, along with seven spherical white eggs. He re-created the scene in one of his glass cases, with part of the artificial bank opened up to reveal the typical underground nesting chamber the birds would excavate. Viewers could inspect this by going around to one side of the case, where a hand-written label stated that the nest, made of fish bones, and the eggs it contained were taken by Potter in 1878.

The case is richly decorated with artificial ivy leaves and other vegetation, which enhance the interest and complexity. A moorhen family was added, along with a few other appropriate species. Old guidebooks mention a hidden stoat creeping up on a scared leveret. Although there is now no sign of the stoat, a tiny timid-looking mouse can be seen peeping out from behind a tree trunk. As with Potter's other large cases, there is plenty of intricate detail here, and much to be learned—or shown to children—with closer inspection.

KINGFISHERS NEST AND EGGS
To be seen in end of case.
Nest made of fish bones.
Taken by: W. Potter.
1878

• CHAPTER 3 •

WALTER POTTER'S MUSEUM

BRAMBER (1861–1972)

**W**ell into old age, and long after the death of his wife, Walter Potter continued to greet visitors to the museum, which remained open during World War I. An item in *The People* on January 4, 1914, referred to a "museum never to be forgotten." Here, it said, "people may fail to recognise in the old gentleman, who is often to be seen seated near the door, a genius who has created a fairyland of nursery rhymes and who not withstanding his 78 years is as much wrapt up in the tale of Nature as he was some 60 years ago when he started his life's work."

The old building to the left in the pub yard, which had previously housed the museum, was made into a tearoom in 1954, enhancing the appeal of a visit to Bramber and providing additional income for the museum.

The jar of conjoined twin pigs that was in the entrance room at Bramber Museum.

Sadly, Walter never finished his last taxidermical scene, *The Squirrels' Court, with Judge and Jury*. In autumn 1914, he suffered a minor stroke from which he never fully recovered. He died on May 1, 1918, aged eighty-two.

Walter Jr., a solicitor's clerk, inherited half of his father's estate (valued at £1,189/6/9d, about fifty percent more than his publican grandfather's), but was evidently unwilling to take on responsibility for the museum. His sister Minnie inherited the museum and ran it with her husband, Edgar Weller Collins, for at least twenty years. Edgar enlarged the collection and produced a new guidebook. As part of his promotional activities, he kept a long wooden box of forty-five magic-lantern slides, which he probably used when giving illustrated talks about the museum at local schools, workingmen's clubs, and social gatherings.

During World War II the museum remained open at least part of the time, with schoolchildren among the visitors. Canadian soldiers were bil-

A still from a 1965 Pathé News film.

leted at Bramber Villa, and they would have spread news of their remark-able circumstances to disbelieving friends and relatives across the Atlantic.

Edgar Walter Collins (known as "Eddie"), Minnie and Edgar Collins's son, had a distinguished record of war service, pioneering radar systems. After the war he declined offers of employment with the electronics firms EMI and Philips to follow his mother's wishes and help her look after the museum, his father having died in 1938. Eddie ran the museum as a fa-mous and successful tourist attraction and seems to have been well suited to the job. In fact, he had been involved probably even before the war; in 1932 he was featured in a *Worthing Herald* article about the museum that de-scribed him as a very jolly person, "a showman to his fingertips." Accord-ing to Eddie, women visitors' favorite exhibit was *The Kittens' Wedding*, while men were fascinated by the freaks; children praised *The Death & Burial of Cock Robin* "every time." His mother continued to help out behind the counter, as she had done for many years, until she died in January 1965.

During the winter, the museum opened only sporadically, but in the

A display of photographs recording a visit to Bramber Museum by the 1950s film and TV personality Diana Dors, Britain's answer to Marilyn Monroe. She signed it, with a dedication to Eddie Collins.

The sale at Jamaica Inn was perhaps the most high-profile event Bonhams had ever organized. The auction catalogue sold out in spite of its high price, and the sale was spread over a two-day period, September 23 and 24, 2003. At the last moment, the contemporary artist Damien Hirst was said to have offered a million pounds to save the collection for the nation. Unfortunately, the offer came too late, and although it was reported in the media, it seems that the owners were unaware of it, so the collection was sold piecemeal by auction.

The sale attracted more than four hundred people, including dealers, media folk, people from the art world, and collectors, despite the relative inaccessibility of the location on Bodmin Moor. A few minor objects were purchased by Steyning Museum and returned to Sussex. The pop artist Sir Peter Blake bought *House That Jack Built* and some smaller items.

The Kittens' Wedding went to America (for £18,000, plus buyer's premium), as did *Monkey Riding a Goat*. While *Kittens' Tea and Croquet Party* sold for a hammer price of £16,000, some of the other large tableaux fetched considerably less, under £10,000 each. The most famous of them, *The Death & Burial of Cock Robin*, was sold to the Victorian Taxidermy Company for a hammer price of £20,000, the highest in the sale.

The front cover of the Bonhams auction catalog.

THE AFTERMATH

Potter's collection was no more. After nearly 150 years of delighting and mystifying more than two million visitors, this unique assemblage was scattered across the country and overseas.

CHAPTER 4

EPHEMERA

Potter's museum charmed and delighted locals and tourists alike for almost 150 years. Although it was most famous for its anthropomorphic tableaux, several other pieces captured the popular imagination. One favorite with visitors, and the subject of one of the museum's colored postcards, was *Monkey Riding a Goat*—a vervet monkey depicted rather improbably carrying a riding crop and seated astride a goat. According to the Bramber Museum guidebook, which immortalizes Potter's own explanation, both animals had come to an untimely end. The monkey, probably an escaped pet, reportedly died of shock

W.P.235. KITTEN WITH 4 EYES, 2 FACES & 2 MOUTHS.

IT WAS BORN AT BROADWATER, WORTHING, & LIVED 7 DAYS

(across spread, lower right)
Rabbit with Tusks
(actually overgrown incisors)
was featured on one of Bramber
Museum's early postcards.

Potter's pet canary, one of his first
bird pieces, was mounted in 1854,
when he was nineteen. The ruins of
Bramber Castle can be seen in the
background; Potter's trade label is
in the lower right–hand corner.

Postcards were obvious and inexpensive souvenirs of a visit to Potter's museum, and many of them were sold.

BRAMBER MUSEUM. KITTEN WITH 8 LEGS & 2 TAILS.

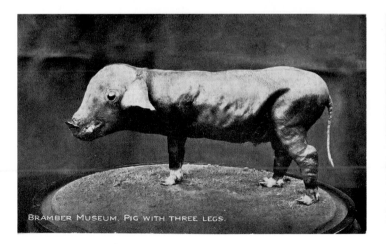

BRAMBER MUSEUM. PIG WITH THREE LEGS.

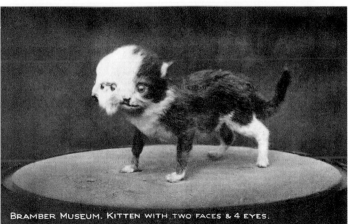

BRAMBER MUSEUM. KITTEN WITH TWO FACES & 4 EYES.

BRAMBER MUSEUM.

Kitten with eight legs & two tails.

BRAMBER MUSEUM.

Hen with four legs.

BRAMBER MUSEUM.

Four legged chick.

Four legged, four winged duckling.

BRAMBER MUSEUM

Athletic Toads.

BRAMBER MUSEUM.

Rabbit with perfected teeth.

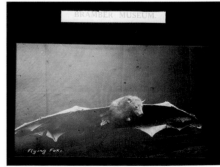

BRAMBER MUSEUM.

Flying Fox.

*These three-by-three-inch glass-plate magic-lantern slides of typical exhibits were used for illustrated talks
at local schools and workingmen's clubs and at various social gatherings.*

ACKNOWLEDGMENTS

The author would like to thank John and Wendy Watts for their enormous generosity over many years and for the help that they and James Cartland provided in respect of the earlier edition of this book. Special thanks also to James Atkins, Jon Baddeley, Laetitia Barbier, Sir Peter Blake, James Brett, Toby Clarkson, James Cranfield, Kate Davies, Robert Devcic, John Drysdale, Errol Fuller, Candice Groot, Charlotte Hanlon, Ben and Lucy Hard, Damien Hirst, Carol and Ron Holzner, Eric Huang, Susan Jeiven, Vadim Kosmos, Lauren Levato, David McComb, Evan Michelson, Jana Miller, Mark Pilkington, Skye Enyeart Rust, Alexis Turner, Cathy Ward, John Whitenight and Frederick LaValley, Viktor Wynd, and Mike Zohn. Particular thanks to J. R. Pepper and G. F. Newland for their help with image corrections.

PHOTOGRAPHY CREDITS

pp. 5 (top), 18, 102 (top): Courtesy Bonhams London
pp. 9, 17, 19 (top), 20, 22–24, 49–55, 68–71, 76–97, 120: Joanna Ebenstein
pp. 26 (bottom), 46, 56–57, 116, 125: Pat Morris
pp. 72–75, 124 (bottom left): Courtesy Murderme Collection
p. 102 (bottom): British Pathé Ltd
pp. 122, 123 (top left): John Drysdale
p. 124 (top right): Collection of John Whitenight and Frederick LaValley, photograph by Alan Kolc
p. 124 (top left): Collection of Carol and Ron Holzner; photograph by Chris Bradley
p. 124 (bottom right): James Cranfield, of Cranfield's Curiosity Cabinet, private collection

ABOUT THE AUTHORS

DR. PAT MORRIS is a professional biologist, formerly senior lecturer in zoology at Royal Holloway, University of London. He specializes in mammal ecology, particularly hedgehogs and dormice, and has traveled to more than thirty countries, including most of the United States, for research. Morris has published at least 150 scientific papers and magazine articles and some twenty books on natural history topics. His lifelong hobby interest has been the history and practice of taxidermy; he has written nine books on the subject, including *A History of Taxidermy: Art, Science and Bad Taste* (MPM Publishing, 2010). He first visited Potter's museum in Bramber as a schoolboy around 1955 and some thirty years later became a technical advisor to its owners. With their help, he gained an unrivaled knowledge of Potter's work, and in 2008 published *Walter Potter and His Museum of Curious Taxidermy*, which records a unique collection now dispersed by its sale in 2003.

JOANNA EBENSTEIN is an artist, designer, events producer, and independent scholar based in Brooklyn, New York. Her work revolves around hidden and private collections, and artifacts that fall through the cracks of disciplines or the temper of the times. She runs the Morbid Anatomy blog, dedicated to surveying "the interstices of art and medicine, death and culture," and the Morbid Anatomy Library, which makes available to the public her collection of art, ephemera, books, and curiosities that show where death and beauty intersect. She also organizes the "Morbid Anatomy Presents" series of lectures, workshops, and exhibitions around the world; by far the most popular class offered is anthropomorphic taxidermy in the style of Walter Potter. You can find out more at http://morbidanatomy.blogspot.com.

DISCOVER MUCH MORE ABOUT WALTER POTTER'S CURIOUS WORLD OF TAXIDERMY AT WWW.WALTERPOTTERTAXIDERMY.COM.